FAST TRACK

An Inside Guide to Car and Motorcycle Racing

Written by Jordan Deutsch
Photos by Jeffrey E. Blackman

Parachute Press, Inc.

Parachute Press, Inc.
200 Fifth Avenue, Room 461
New York, New York 10010

First printing August 1987
Printed in the U.S.A.

The author wishes to thank the following individuals, organizations, and publications in the preparation of this manuscript:

Lawrence Lockhart
Margaret I. Reysen

***

American Motorcyclist Association
Championship Auto Racing Teams
Continental Motosport Club
International Motor Sports Association
National Association for Stock Car Auto Racing
National Hot Rod Association

***

Cycle magazine
Dirt Wheels magazine
Motocross Action magazine
Popular Mechanics magazine
Road Track magazine
Sports Illustrated magazine

CONTENTS

PART ONE:

AUTO RACING

INTRODUCTION

"Gentlemen, Start Your Engines!"

But first we suggest you put on your helmet and gloves and buckle your safety harness. Now try to imagine coming within a millimeter of disaster as you squeeze past two tons of high-powered metal in the last lap on a sizzling superspeedway—at 200 mph!

Did you ever wonder what it's like to push a machine to its ultimate maximum before tens of thousands of screaming fans and have a tire suddenly explode and $100,000 worth of precision race car go spinning wildly off the track? Or to ride a steel monster so fast it needs a parachute to stop? Or to change four wheels, refuel, clean a windshield, and give the driver a cold drink, all in under 30 seconds?

Welcome to the fast-track world of auto racing!

It's a complicated place. It's gasoline, guts, speed and skill, lightning reflexes, and split-second decisions. It's where mistakes mean not just lost money, but crippling injury and sometimes even death. It's also a place that's open to anyone willing and talented enough to gamble for success or failure at high-stake risks. For those who succeed, the rewards are great. For those who watch and fantasize being behind the wheel, the thrills and excitement are fast and furious.

To discover what this world of speed is really like means taking a look at the types of cars—not only what's on the outside, but the nuts and bolts of the incredible engines beneath the hoods. You'll find out where it all started, what races and tracks are the "jewels" in the championship crowns, and meet the superstars who drive these fantastic machines. There's also an insider's view of the action that takes place in the pits during an actual race. And there's a cold, hard look at what happens when the machines go haywire and crash—and the kind of courageous determination it takes to survive and return for another go at the track.

Beyond the big events that draw millions of fans there are the offbeat and smaller races and cars which have their own special followings—from the parking lots of America to the plains of Africa.

Ready to begin? In those famous words first spoken a long time ago, "Gentlemen, start your engines!"

THE DIFFERENT KINDS OF AUTO RACING

GRAND PRIX

This kind of racing uses the specially designed Formula One car. Some Grand Prix races are run on regular roads and others on specially built courses. Most of the races are held in Europe and are 200 miles long. The world championship is decided by total points won in a series of 17 races.

INDY CARS

Indy cars are similar to Formula One cars. They are the kind of cars that are used in the Indianapolis 500. The Indy car championship consists of a series of 14 races, the most famous of which is the Indy 500. The driver who earns the most points is the champion.

STOCK CARS

These are cars that are bought in an automobile showroom and rebuilt from the ground up for racing. This is a truly American form of the sport. There are 29 races to decide the champion. As in Grand Prix and Indy, the driver who earns the most points in the 29 races wins the title.

SPORTS CARS

This kind of racing uses cars such as Porsches, Jaguars, Datsuns, and Corvettes, among others. Using a point system, drivers compete in 21 races for the championship.

DRAG CARS

These cars are designed for high-speed racing over a distance of a quarter mile. The winner of each race is decided by a series of elimination time trials. Dragsters are so fast they need a parachute to stop.

HOW AUTO RACING GOT STARTED

GRAND PRIX AUTO RACING

The first official auto race took place nearly 100 years ago. It wasn't anything like the high-speed excitement we see today. In fact, it was closer to a Sunday drive in the country.

The first race was held in Paris, France. It started in Paris, went to Bordeaux, and then returned to Paris two days later. The year was 1895 and the average speed was a whopping 15 miles per hour!

The event caused interest and it quickly spread all over Europe. The FIA (International Auto Federation) was formed to govern the races, and eleven years later the first true Grand Prix (pronounced "pre") was held on a course near Le Mans, France. Instead of an oval track, the drivers had to deal with hairpin turns and whatever other hazards the track had to offer.

The main thing that has changed between then and now is the cars. The original racers would have been awestruck by the cars used in Grand Prix racing today—the mighty Formula Ones.

Other things have changed as well. In the beginning the races belonged exclusively to the rich and racing was known as a "gentleman's sport." Although Grand Prix is still considered the most "high class" of all types of racing, it is open to anyone with guts and determination enough to try. It has also branched out to other countries. The Grand Prix races which determine the world champion—17 races in all—include races run in Australia, Brazil, Japan, France, Canada, England, Germany, and even behind the iron curtain in Hungary. The one Grand Prix race held in the United States now takes place in the Motor City of Detroit. (It used to be held in Watkins Glen, New York.)

Most of the races are still run in Europe and each course has its own fabled history. What is really unique about Grand Prix racing is the great challenge it offers from country to country. In Mexico City, where the altitude is 7300 feet above sea level, drivers have to worry about overheated engines. In Belgium there's a hairpin turn so tight that speeds above 30 mph are considered unsafe!

The toughest and most popular course is the Monaco Grand Prix, held in the city of Monte Carlo in the south of France. The drivers call it the "race of a thousand corners." It is two-and-a-half miles of turns and straightaways.

The story of racing in America has a different background. In 1909 a young businessman turned 320 acres of Indiana farmland into what has become the most famous oval in the world—the Indianapolis Motor Speedway. The race run over it also became the richest, with prize money of four million dollars in 1986, and the most popular, with over 500,000 people going every year to watch the 500-mile event.

The first Indy race was held on Memorial Day in 1911, and was won by Ray Harroun at an average speed of 74.5 mph. Except for the war years of the 1940s, it has been an annual event ever since.

Bobby Rahal won it in 1986 at an average speed of 170.7 mph. The two-and-a-half mile track, nicknamed the Brickyard because it was originally paved with bricks, is a grueling 200-lap test of speed, concentration, and endurance. One of the more famous traditions of the Indy—the world's oldest continuously operating track—is that instead of champagne, the winner toasts his victory with a quart of milk!

But while winning the Indy 500 is a prize in itself, it is only a "jewel" in the champion's crown and one of the races to decide the championship. To win the championship on the Indy circuit—which is known as CART (Championship Auto Racing Teams)—you have to prove your ability on 13 other tracks, which include 500- and 200-mile races. The competition is spread out from Long Beach, California, home of the Toyota Grand Prix, to Miami, Florida, where the

Nissan Indy Challenge is held. There's even a race in Canada, which takes place at the Sanair Super Speedway oval in Quebec.

The CART series has not only attracted most of the top drivers in the United States but many European racers as well. Aside from the honor, one of the reasons it attracts many Grand Prix drivers is that the Indy car, as it is known, is almost a duplicate of the European Formula One. (You'll find the difference in Chapter Three, "Nuts and Bolts.")

STOCK CAR RACING

While Indy may have the longest history of any car race in this country, it is not the most American example of the sport. That honor belongs to stock car racing and the tracks known as "Thunder Road."

Like jazz and baseball, stock car racing is 100% born and raised in the USA. It is American drivers in American-made cars. They race more miles than drivers in any other form of motor sport.

Under the direction of NASCAR (National Association for Stock Car Racing) the sport attracts over 15 million fans in its many events spread out over nine divisions. That figure is unmatched by any other kind of auto racing. CART may have paid out more money—$15.5 million in 1986, compared to NASCAR's $15.3 million—but the stock circuit still gets the nod for being the people's choice.

Stock car racing was started on dusty dirt tracks deep in the heart of Dixie and was open to anyone who had a Chevy or Ford or any other factory-built car sitting in their driveway. To say the least, it was a rough-and-tumble weekend circus put on in fields better suited to growing cotton than to racing.

That was before NASCAR was formed in Daytona Beach, Florida, in 1947. A year later the organization staged its first official race and brought order by making drivers comply with a set of rules. They set guidelines on what kind of cars could compete, how they were to be driven, and what safety standards had to be met. NASCAR also set up a point system, guaranteed the prize money, and promoted it as a "family sport" to give the stocks some respectability after its ragtag beginning.

The tracks were still of dirt—or even a sandy beach, like the old track at Daytona—until Darlington Speedway opened in South Carolina. That was in 1950, the year that ushered in a new era of paved tracks, higher speed, and more money. Today hundreds of drivers race on dozens of tracks from coast to coast. But the focus of what is known as "Southern-fried racing" is still below the Mason-Dixon Line. It is the home of 10 of the 15 speedways that host NASCAR's Winston Cup Series.

It's a tough grind that in 1987 will see the cream of NASCAR drivers compete in 29 events, trying to chalk up points that range from 175 for a win to 43 for the 40th-place finisher. As with CART's system, drivers who lead the most laps in the Winston Cup Series get bonus points. In addition to what a driver may earn in individual races, the one with the most points wins the Winston Cup and a half-million dollars in bonus money.

To add some more whipped cream to the pie, NASCAR also offers another million dollars to any driver who wins three of the four races known as the "crown jewels." They are the Daytona 500, the Winston 500 at Alabama's Talladega Speedway, the Coca-Cola 600 at Charlotte, North Carolina, and the Southern 500 at Darlington. It's a far cry from the days before NASCAR, when the winner of a race usually got $20!

SPORTS CAR RACING

Beyond "Thunder Road" is the sports car circuit. It is governed by a group called IMSA (International Motor Sports Association) and uses the theme "racing with a difference." From its humble beginning in 1969, when the first event drew 348 spectators, IMSA racing has grown by leaps and bounds. Today, it draws tens of thousands of fans and entries from all over the world. There are four divisions in which the drivers compete for the crown and a share in the bonus money, a figure that has climbed to a record $700,000 in 1987.

This exciting brand of auto racing includes a schedule of 21 races. The series includes four races that are run through the city streets of Miami and West Palm Beach, Florida, San Antonio, Texas, and Columbus, Ohio.

The most unusual is the Columbus event. It is the only race in the world in which a river (the Scioto) is crossed twice. There are also three endurance races. The "12 Hours of Sebring," run in Florida, is probably the most famous of any IMSA race. In 1986 it lived up to its reputation for being the "wildest and wackiest" of the season. The winning car, a Porsche 962, lost its left front wheel in the final turn and still made it across the finish line!

DRAG RACING

Last, but not least, in the world of major auto racing is the sport that was once called a "public menace." That's when it was known as "hot rodding." From the old airstrips—the best place a driver could test the speed of his car—came the birth of what we now know as drag racing. It is the simplest, fastest, and in many ways the most exciting. The entire race is run on a ¼-mile straightaway, two cars at a time, with speeds in the 270-mph range!

As with NASCAR, the sport became respectable when an organization, NHRA (the National Hot Rod Association), was formed in 1954. The first national championship was held on an abandoned airfield in Kansas and the winner received nothing more than a trophy. The "Nationals" finally found a permanent home in 1961 in a 260-acre "showcase" in Clermont, Indiana. The purse there is now one of the highest of any race in the world—a cool one million dollars!

These expensive, high-tech machines, which sometimes look more like something from outer space, also include more than 150 classes of cars. They compete in 11 categories at over 3000 races on

NHRA-member tracks across the country. There's a schedule of 15 events for what are considered the "purely professional category" of cars: Top Fuel, Funny Car, and Pro Stock. The winners take home a trophy and a barrel of prize money—not bad for a sport that goes from start to finish in less than 5.3 seconds.

2

RACING SUPERSTARS

STOCK CAR DRIVERS

The man the fans scream for most is probably more recognized for his famous Number 43 than he might be for his name. It's **Richard Petty**, better known as "King Richard."

He has a quick smile for anyone he meets and a "down home" manner which will put a stranger at ease. That's off the track. Once he's behind the wheel, it's another story. The reason they call Petty "King" is because he's won more races (200) than any other driver in stock car history. To go along with that impressive record are present earnings of over 10 million dollars and a record seven Winston Cup driving championships.

Petty, a native of North Carolina, began his stock career with NASCAR in 1958, following in the foot-steps of his father, Lee, who entered racing at the age of 35 and racked up 54 victories.

"King Richard" may be slowing down a bit at age 51. For the first time in many years he failed to make the top-ten list in 1985 and 1986. But during those years there was still a Petty on the list. It was his son, Kyle, who broke into the circuit in 1979. Whatever "King Richard" might do in the future, there's certain to be a Petty in stock car racing into the 21st century!

While Richard Petty might be everyone's favorite, stock car competitor **Darrell Waltrip** tips the scales on the other end for many fans. Although there are many in his corner, there is likely to be the same number who do not like him. The main reason is his criticism of the NASCAR point system for determining champions.

Waltrip, who started his racing career at age 12 in supermarket parking lots, has all the credentials in the world for speaking his mind. He's won two NASCAR championships and three Driver of the Year awards.

The most respected driver on the stock car circuit is **Bill Elliott**. Unlike many drivers who do little more than drive the car their team has built, Elliott works on the cars he drives.

Racing is a family affair for Elliott. Aside from Bill, there are 11 other Elliotts who live and work together to make sure their famous T-Bird goes from start to finish without a hitch. Bill is another favorite of the fans, having been voted Most Popular Driver for the past three years (1984–1986).

But as good as all these drivers are, the best in

1986 was **Dale Earnhardt**. He nailed down his second NASCAR championship and won over a million dollars in the process! While Earnhardt was burning up the ovals, rookie **Alan Kulwicki** overcame a lot of bad luck in his first season to be named the circuit's top rookie. His chief rival for the honor was **Mike Waltrip**, Darrell's younger brother.

No list of stock car champions would be complete without the names **Bobby Allison** and **Cale Yarborough**. Allison won the top NASCAR honors in 1983 and Yarborough was the only driver to win the championship for three straight years, 1976–1978.

Another name that is very much a part of the stock car world is **Wendell Scott**. What Scott did in the 1960s was harder than winning a 500 event. He became the first black man to crack the race barrier and had the honor of having Richard Pryor portray his life story in the movie *Greased Lightning*.

INDY AND GRAND PRIX DRIVERS

There is little that **A.J. Foyt**—or "Super Tex," as he's known—hasn't accomplished on the track. He's not only won the Indy 500 a record four times, but has added the Daytona 500, one of the jewels in the stock crown, to his list of victories. The most impressive feat for this versatile superstar, who still competes in Indy 500 main events at age 53, was winning the 24 Hours of Le Mans. It is one of the toughest endurance races in the world in one of the toughest circuits in the world—the Grand Prix—a class that uses the powerful Formula One car and is basically considered a European sport.

The only other man who might be as durable as Foyt is **Mario Andretti**. He's the only racer ever to be selected "Driver of the Year" in three decades—the 1960s, 1970s, and 1980s—and the only one to win both the World Grand Prix Championship and the CART title. Mario, who started life in Trieste, Italy, and who built his first car in 1948 with his twin brother, **Aldo**, is the cornerstone of what promises to become a racing dynasty. In 1983 his son **Michael Andretti** broke into the Indy car circuit, and not far behind was Mike's kid brother, **Jeff Andretti**, who's quickly coming up the through the ranks following his success in the smaller Super Vee class. To top it off, there is **John Andretti**, Aldo's son, who races on the IMSA circuit.

While the younger Andrettis might have their names on the Indy championship series cup in the future, another famous racer's son—**Al Unser, Jr.**—is making today's headlines. "Big Al" and "Little Al" are the hottest duo in Indy cars. And if you're wondering if they're competitive with each other, just take a look at the 1985 CART season.

Going into the last race at Miami in the Indy Challenge, **Al Unser, Sr.** led Al Jr. by one point. But with four laps to go Al Sr. passed **Roberto Moreno** to capture fourth place. "Little Al" finished ahead of his dad, but third place still wasn't enough to win the cup. He finished with 150 points to his father's 151, the closest points fight in modern Indy car history! It was Al Sr.'s third championship, and at age

48 he became the oldest driver to win the title. If Al Jr. had won, he'd have been the youngest at age 23. The Unsers are also a "family act" that has a long history. It includes Al's father, two uncles, and two brothers, Bobby and Jerry. One of racing's tragedies occurred when **Jerry Unser** was killed at Indy in 1958. But the Unser spirit continues, as is witnessed by Al Sr.'s mother, Mary Catherine, who started the Unser Green Chili Feast, an annual prerace event at the famous Indy 500.

In 1987 Al Unser, Sr. showed his stuff once again. He won the Indy 500, making it his second Indy 500 win.

Another superstar on the Indy circuit is **"Broadway Danny" Sullivan**. Unlike Al Unser, Jr., whose father taught him to drive when he was nine, Sullivan learned his trade at the Jim Russell School of Motor Racing in England. Danny attended the University of Kentucky for two semesters, but his desire to race for a living soon took him to New York City, where he worked as a janitor, cab driver, and waiter. Other jobs elsewhere included lumber jack, sod cutter, and chicken-ranch hand. It was on Danny's 21st birthday that Dr. Frank Fakner, a longtime SCCA official, saw the promise in Sullivan's driving ability and paid his tuition to the Russell school. His big break came while he was living in the back of an old car in England—a chance to race Formula Fords. He broke into Indy driving in 1982 and won the Indy 500 in 1985, becoming one of the quickest millionaires in auto racing history. He is considered one of Indy's flashiest drivers, with a personality that matches his prowess on the track. After all, how many other drivers got to appear in an episode of *Miami Vice*?

From flashiest to bravest—**Tom Sneva**, the first man to break the 200-mph/lap barrier, a feat he accomplished in 1977. That was also the year he won the first of two straight driving championships.

Sneva, known as "Tom Terrific" for his courage on the track, first broke into Indy racing in 1971. Before that he was a math and physical ed teacher and junior high school principal. He was also a high school and college basketball player. Sneva, still among the leaders in CART racing, is helped by his wife, Sharon, who serves as his timer and scorer. Two brothers in the sport, Jerry and Blaine, currently race modified and sprints. Jerry was the Indy 500 Rookie of the Year in 1977.

When "Tom Terrific" is not driving his high-speed machines, he is often seen behind the wheel of his 1927 Model T street rod, one of many cars in his personal collection.

When it comes to consistency and sheer driving ability, most drivers and fans will name **Rick Mears** as the man who heads these categories. Of all the stories about Mears's ability, the most famous is that he first got behind the wheel of an Indy car in 1976 and it wasn't until 1984 that he had his first accident. It almost cost him his life, but he returned in 1985 to take his second Indy 500 (the first was in 1979).

Mears has also won the Indy car championship three times. His older brother, Roger, has driven

Indy cars but is better known for his off-road racing career.

Mears lives in Bakersfield, California, where a local fan club, known as the "Mears Gang," was formed in his honor. The man who collects steering wheels, owns and flies an ultralight aircraft, and works with remote cars and planes is also highly regarded by fellow drivers. As Al Unser, Sr., said when accepting his trophy at the CART Awards Banquet in 1985: "I'd like Rick to accept and carry the Number One next year. He's the guy that earned it."

Another driver quickly entering the class of these superstars is 35-year-old **Bobby Rahal**. For a man who decided not to become a fighter pilot because of poor eyesight, he saw well enough to take his first Indy 500 in 1986 after breaking into CART in 1982.

In a sport dominated by men, **Janet Guthrie** is now as much a part of CART history as any of the speed records. Janet worked against the odds to become the first woman to qualify for the Indy 500, something she accomplished in 1976.

SPORTS CAR DRIVERS

In road racing, which uses souped-up sports cars and is sanctioned by IMSA, the top name belongs to **Al Holbert**, who was Camel GT Overall Champion three out of the past four years. Holbert turned the trick with his Lowenbrau Special Porsche 962.

Sports car racing also attracts its share of celebrities. They include **Paul Newman** and **James Gar-**

ner, who both have made movies about racing (*Winning* and *Grand Prix*). Newman's sidekick in the movie *The Color of Money* was **Tom Cruise**, who also includes sports car racing as one of his true "loves." Rounding out the celebrity circuit is singer/writer **Christopher Cross**, **Mark Knopfeler** of the rock group Dire Straits, and Olympic gold medal winner **Bruce Jenner**.

DRAG RACERS

But, of course, you can't talk about racing drivers without mentioning the names of some very special people. They might not be known for their ability to take the turns, but they are the favorites of tens of thousands who follow the NHRA drag circuit.

Number One in this exciting sport of high-speed cars that are like quarter-mile rockets is **Don Garlits**. He is, indeed, the king of all he surveys. The Tampa, Florida, native known as "Big Daddy" is considered by many to be the father of modern competitive drag racing. He has more wins, records, titles, and championships than any other driver in NHRA history.

Part of what makes "Big Daddy" Garlits so special is that he's brought more ideas to the sport than any other competitor. And despite having some bad accidents—one recently—he continues to burn up his younger rivals at age 56.

Some of these rivals include **Darrell Gwynn** and **Shirley ("Cha Cha") Muldowney**. While Gwynn is cast as "the young man who's trying," Muldowney holds the distinction of being the first woman to show that it's not just a man's sport. She's proved this by her courage on the track and off, where she is making an incredible comeback following a near-fatal accident.

3

UNDER THE HOOD

Not all the the excitement in motor sports takes place on the track. There's even more action where you can't see it—under the hood. We're going to take a look at some of the things that make a race car so special, from what they look like to what they cost. And, most important, what it takes to get them moving past the 200-mph mark.

GRAND PRIX AND INDY CARS

The kind of cars that are used in Grand Prix racing and in the Indy circuit might be called "almost identical twins." In the Grand Prix they use the Formula One car while Indy uses a similar car known as the Indy car. One thing for certain, they both look like they can fly. Their sleek body is long and low, streamlined to knife through space. Where other cars have bumpers, these high-tech inventions have thin "wings" attached to the front and back. They are known as airfoils, or "spoilers," and are used to increase handling control and cornering speed. In the Indy car, the power source that makes these wings necessary is a turbocharged V-6 or V-8 engine. They are gleaming masterpieces of the mechanic's art that can go from zero to 80 mph in four seconds and come to a complete stop in a distance of 123 feet.

There are no fenders, but 16-inch-wide tires in the rear provide better traction (they heat up after a few laps and get a firm grip on the track) and the front wheels are narrow to improve steering. All four tires are treadless and the wheels have large disc brakes. The length and width (15 ½ feet long and 6 ½ feet wide) are close to the size of an averge passenger car. But Indy and Grand Prix cars stand only 3 feet high and clear the ground at 2 ½ to 3 inches—hardly enough room to get your fist under!

The bodies are lightweight shells made of aluminum and they must be crash-tested by the manufacturer, just as the makers of regular cars must do. The finished product, complete with engine, weighs about the same as a little Volkswagen Beetle—1550 pounds—but has a price tag of up to $300,000!

The snug little cockpit sits in front of the engine—most are only 18 inches wide—and has just enough room for the driver and the controls. For protection, a fire extinguisher, safety harness, and roll bar are standard equipment. For further protection against fire in the event of a crash, a rubber "in-

31

ner tube" is fitted inside the gas tank.

The engines and bodies for these cars are made by many different companies, but the favorites are body by March or Lola and engine by Cosworth—all British products. At Indy, this combination racked up nine wins in a row (1978–1986), a record second only to the one set by an American-made engine that has been around the Indy circuit since 1921, the legendary Offenhauser. It accounted for a total of 28 wins at the Indy 500. Oddly enough, the Cosworth engine may soon be replaced by an American brand since the first two starting positions in the 1986 Indy 500 had the Buick trademark under the hood.

Where the Grand Prix and Indy cars differ is in the kind of fuel they use. Formula One, Grand Prix cars burn gasoline and Indy cars run on a mixture called methanol.

As much as 20,000 gallons of methanol may be used in a single Indy race and up to 200,000 gallons in one season. The Indy car is limited to a 40-gallon tank. And one thing the engine does not deliver is "more miles to the gallon"—only 1.8 mpg (miles per gallon)!

Most Grand Prix cars do only a little better on gasoline at 4 mpg. But their tanks are limited to 50 gallons and it is not uncommon for a Grand Prix driver to run out of gas in a 200-mile event and be forced to push his car across the finish line.

STOCK CARS

Just as an Indy or Formula One car is built from the ground up, for racing, the reverse is true for a stock car. On the surface the cars that race at NASCAR tracks such as Daytona and Charlotte might look like the ones you see in your local auto dealer's showroom. But rest assured that everything has been changed, moved around, or taken out altogether.

The process involves starting out with a regular American car—which cannot be more than two years old—and then removing the headlights and taillights and all other parts that could vibrate loose during a race. The shape and measurement of the original body must remain the same. No streamlining is allowed. The "skeleton" is then completely reinforced, the steel roll cage is added along with a shoulder harness, padded steering wheel, and a nylon web "net" in the driver's window. Extra padding on the right side of the seat is also added for comfort and safety, since constant left turns on the NASCAR tracks force the driver's body to the right. Otherwise, a lot of stiff necks would result.

Only gasoline engines can be used in NASCAR racing, generally a V-8 or V-6, although improvements to increase speed are permitted. Fuel injection and automatic transmissions are barred throughout the circuit and the same kind of rubber gas tank used on Indy and Formula One cars is required. The tank is limited to 22 gallons and a stock car must start under its own power (Formula One and Indy cars use a separate battery). Also, all tires have to be the same size. Most important is that the car is inspected before every race and the engine is sealed by NASCAR officials.

Ready to race, the finished package will crank out 650 horsepower, weigh 3700 pounds, and cost in the neighborhood of $65,000, with a quarter of the money going into the engine alone. Costs, including a backup car, spare engines and parts, plus crew salaries, means a top NASCAR team may easily spend $2.5 million in one season of racing.

DRAG RACERS

Probably no form of the sport has changed its look more than drag racing. Back in the late 1940s the cars were souped-up jalopies that could be driven on the street as well as on the track. Those early "hot rods" have given way to what are now known as Top Fuel, Pro Stock, and the Funny Car, drag racing's three main classes.

A Top Fuel dragster, fastest of the three, is little more than a monster engine, a driver's seat, bicycle-type wheels in the front, and huge wheels in the rear, all of it strung together on a frame made of chrome-steel tubing. Overall length of a typical dragster is about 20 feet, and one large wing is mounted high above the back wheels to help control its path down the straightaway.

The tires are called "slicks" because they have no tread. The oversize rear tires are made of a special soft rubber that becomes gummy and actually sticks to the asphalt after a couple of practice starts.

Top Fuelers run on nitromethane. It has several times the energy of gasoline. By burning this powerful fuel in all-aluminum engines that are custom-built to deliver a whopping 2500 horsepower, it is easy to see why dragsters cover the quarter mile in 5.3 seconds from a standing start and reach speeds of over 270 mph.

Thanks to Don Garlits, who decided to sit in front of the supercharged demon engine instead of behind it, there is now much more safety in racing a dragster. It was also "Big Daddy" who suggested using a parachute to help stop the cars since only the back wheels have brakes.

Unlike the Top Fueler, the average Pro Stock machine resembles a car that you are likely to see on the streets of any city or town. But, again, that's only what meets the eye. Beneath the glossy paint jobs are massive engines that turn these common passenger cars into awesome performers as they complete a quarter-mile race in seven seconds at 190 mph.

Although dragsters are the fastest and Pro Stockers the closest to actual automobiles, the one that packs the stands everywhere is the Funny Car. Funny Cars got their name when some contestants stretched NHRA rules by moving the back wheels further toward the front, lowering the hood, and raising the tail end. This cut down wind resistance and increased speed. With its light fiberglass body the modern Funny Car looks like something out of a sci-fi movie. It can reach speeds of over 260 mph and cover the quarter mile in 5.5 seconds. Unlike dragsters, the engine is in its normal location, so the driver wears a fire-resistant suit and a special mask that filters out fumes—and sometimes fire. And, more often than not, it really protects the driver. When nitromethane explodes, the engine is blown apart and the car covered in flames. Surprisingly, even minor injuries are few.

SPORTS CAR RACING

In the IMSA races, where you can see the exciting and unusual sports cars and others that are more familiar, the top of the line is the class called Grand Touring Prototype (GTP). These fantastic machines seem to have come from another world and look like nothing that will be seen on American highways during this century. They have full bodies with sloping fenders that nearly touch the ground, headlights, windshield wipers, two-way radios, and even a special method for keeping the driver cool in the cockpits—which heat up to 135 degrees during a race.

Under their coveralls and racing helmets, GTP drivers wear unique vests and caps that circulates cold water kept in a chest on the cockpit floor. Rightly known as the "leading edge of auto racing," IMSA's GTP cars point the way to the future of motor sports worldwide.

4

PIT STOPS!

"The 27.6-Second Tornado"

If you can imagine pulling into a gas station and having your tank filled, every tire changed, and even getting your windshield cleaned, all in under 30 seconds, then you have a pretty good idea of what takes place during a pit stop. Of course, it takes more than one or two men to pull off this instant miracle. It takes a well-trained pit crew that combines teamwork, training, and timing. In fact, it's such an important operation that no race is won without it.

Where did the idea for pit crews begin? To find the answer we have to go all the way back to 1911. That was the year of the first Indy 500. A young automotive engineer by the name of Ray Harroun was entered in the race. What he did was to carefully measure the tread wear on each of the four big tires after each practice run. Harroun knew that less wear meant fewer stops for replacements.

When the actual race began, Harroun had his strategy. He would maintain a steady pace in the grueling contest and get the most mileage out of his rubber. Harroun was leading when another driver overtook his Marmon Wasp with only 24 laps to go. But he was determined to stick to his plan and he maintained his steady speed. Five laps later he whizzed past the leader and headed straight for victory as the lead car limped off the track for a tire change!

It proved that tires and fuel count most during a race. As any driver will tell you, even a genius can't make an engine rev on a dry tank. Worse yet, bald tires are an invitation to disaster.

To win a race you need three things: a great car, a great driver, and a great pit team. Becoming part of that crew in the pit requires more than the ability to do things fast. You have to be strong and you have to be able to keep the same energy level throughout the race. That means eating salads, fruits, and vegetables instead of junk foods. Also, no soda is kept in the pit. The crew drinks juices, and in many pit areas no sweets are allowed at all!

There are good reasons for all this. A tire weighs close to 90 pounds and a full gas can over 80. If you multiply these numbers by the five pit stops expected during a 500-mile race, you get some idea of why you must be in shape. Being a member of a crew also means constant practice and training. The crew members have to know exactly how far their car will travel on a tank of gas and just how long a tire will hold up against the tremendous strains of heat and pressure. They also have to know about every tool, from the lightweight jacks to the high-speed socket wrenches. And they must be able to act like one man with 20 arms.

Crews are judged on their speed and efficiency. They even have their own competition. In 1967 Unocal 76, the gas company, started sponsoring Pit Crew Championships. The top prize of $6,000 in 1985 and 1986 went to Dale Earnhardt's crew. In 1985 they were able to change all the tires, fill the tank, and wash the windshield in 28.8 seconds. In 1986 they did it in 27.6 seconds! The last team to win back-to-back titles was Richard Petty's crew in 1976–1977.

It's also important to know when to come into the pit. The crew chief or driver can make that decision anytime, but most prefer to wait until a yellow caution flag signals a mishap on the track. That's when the race slows down and passing is forbidden. After a driver slips into the pits he is allowed to resume his position when the pack comes around again. Pitting while the race is running flat-out under a green flag could cost a lap, which is difficult to make up. The whole process is made much easier by constant radio contact between the crew chief and the driver. But radio or not, when the "Meatball Flag" (black with an orange circle) is waved by the crew chief, it means something is wrong (like a smoking engine) and the driver must go straight to the pit!

To give you a good look at the action that takes place in the pits during a race—action that has been described as "a controlled tornado"—we use a NASCAR situation. The rules there only allow six people to service the car. They must stay with their tools behind a wall and are constantly monitored by track officials for violations. Of the six, there's the gas man, his assistant, the jack man, two tire changers, and a tire carrier. When the car comes into the pit, at about 100 mph, it is guided in by one of the crew and must stop exactly at a line near the wall. That crewman must jump back inside the barrier. Then the attack force swarms into action. Here's what happens.

The jack man locates the hoisting pad, marked by an arrow painted below the door. He positions the jack and pumps furiously, raising the entire right side of the car as the gas man swings an 11-gallon can aloft and starts the refueling operation. Meanwhile, the driver stands on the brakes to lock the wheels and the tire carrier holds fresh rubber against the front fender, ready to be mounted. The instant the wheels clear the concrete, he bounds over the jack and delivers the second tire to the rear. Hot lug nuts fly, gas flows, five seconds disappear.

The worn rear "shoe" is yanked off and cleared away by the tire carrier, who then helps fit a new one onto the hub. The jack man does likewise at the front end. The assistant gas man watches for tank overflow and will hand off the empty can for a full one, if needed. Lug nuts glued over stud holes in the rims allow double-quick replacement of used tires, front and rear. . . . Ten seconds, and ticking . . .

Nitrogen-fired impact wrenches zip lugs at 30,000 rpm. The jack man checks that lugs are tightened properly, keeping an eye out for the overflow man's sign that the tank is full. By now, other crew members, using long-handled brushes, have cleaned the windshield and radiator screen and given the driver a cold drink. When the tank's loaded, the gas and tire men leap over the wall. The jack man then lowers the car and signals the driver—GO, GO, GO!

And if the driver and the crew chief haven't traded last-minute instructions, probably nobody's said a word.

Aside from long hours and bruised knuckles and the disappointment of blown engines, there's also the chance of injury or death. Despite all the stiff rules and safety laws, freak accidents still occur in the pits. With all that to consider, plus the fact that a top NASCAR crew chief can command only a fraction of what a driver can earn, you may wonder why anyone would want to do it. Many will tell you it's the excitement or the challenge, or even a mention on the roster at the newly formed Mechanics' Hall of Fame. It's probably a little of all those reasons.

The best reason, though, may have come from Everett "Cotton" Owens, a former driver and pit man: "Drivers get the glory and most of the pay check, deservedly . . . but the real satisfaction goes to the mechanic."

5

INTO THE WALL

Crashes and Comebacks

All racing drivers share one hard fact of life, and that is the cold reality that sooner or later they will crash! It can happen at any time and at any track. It can happen to the best drivers as easily as it can happen to a rookie taking the turns for the first time. To know how dangerous racing is, just consider the regulation that all drivers must have their blood type marked on their helmet!

Most times the drivers are lucky enough to survive even the worst crashes. That's because of special fire-resistant clothing and a cockpit so well designed that it's called the "survival cell." But even the harnesses, nets, and padding that protect drivers from instant death do not mean that they will walk away unharmed or not have to undergo painful surgery and months of rehabilitation. And that's if they're fortunate. Sometimes, even the spectators are the victims. Out-of-control race cars crashing through protective barriers and lunging into crowds have taken their toll over the years.

The worst of these disasters happened in 1952 during the famous 24-hour Le Mans endurance race. With 2 hours left to the race, Pierre Levegh, driving a Mercedes, tried to overtake another driver. But his car nicked the left rear of the Austin-Healy ahead of him and he slammed against an earth-and-wicker barrier where thousands of fans were standing. The impact of the crash shredded the Mercedes, and the engine and front suspension slashed through the crowd like a hot knife through butter. Dozens of fans were seriously injured and Levegh and 80 others were killed!

Sometimes it's not even a case of the driver's ability, since tire blowouts and mechanical failure create havoc on the track. Such was the case of Bill Vukovich, Sr., the Indy champ who lost his life at the 1955 Indy. A car ahead of "the Mad Russian" broke an axle on the 125th lap and set off a chain reaction. Vukie aimed for an opening in the pile of wreckage and the wall, but another car was knocked into his path. Vukovich's car went right over the pack, cleared the wall without touching it, and somersaulted in the air, landing nose first. He died on impact.

Cracking up at high speeds may be a fact of life for all drivers, but it also brings out the yardstick by which courage and determination are measured. Mostly, they chalk it up to experience by saying that they won't make the same mistake the next time out. Cathy Rude, who suffered incredible bone and internal injuries when her Porsche 935 hit another car and exploded at an IMSA event in 1983, returned to the wheel 18 months later. The crash, though, gave her a lot to think about. As she said at the time, "Now that I know the consequences, I have to find out whether I can accept the risks in the same way."

Although all drivers are a breed apart, their reactions following a crash are not always the same. Having your machine explode under you and spending painful months in a hospital take a toll that's almost impossible to imagine. This was the case with Rick Mears, one of the best drivers ever to get behind the wheel of an Indy car.

Mears met with near disaster back in 1984. He was racing his March 84C in a practice race at the Sanair tri-oval in Quebec when he tried to cut around Bobby Rahal in heavy traffic. It was a gamble that didn't pay off. He hit the car that was following closely behind him and was thrown into the guardrail at a speed estimated at 130 mph. The impact was so great that the guardrail tore through the front bulkhead. The accident almost cost Mears the use of his legs. Only the miracle of modern medical science and his own determination to return to the track helped him survive.

Less than 10 months after the crash Mears returned to post a 213-mph practice lap at Indy in preparation for the 500. He didn't win that one, but despite nerve damage that limits his walking to only short distances, he was able to drive far enough and fast enough to win the Pocono 500 later that year.

For Sterling Moss, one of the true Grand Prix legends, the decision to continue racing was different. Moss hit a dirt bank head on at more than 60 mph during a Formula One race in England in 1962. He didn't awake from a coma until a month later and, aside from other serious injuries, his left side was paralyzed for six months. A year later he slid behind the wheel again for a practice lap, but with his vision and concentration still a problem, he knew it was foolish to continue racing. Moss retired as a professional. Oddly enough, when Moss had his accident he wasn't even wearing a seatbelt! This was a practice that many drivers shared back then. Fortunately, it is now a thing of the past.

Whatever the reason for returning to racing after a bad accident—be it ego, money, or that strange challenge to always flirt with death—one of the lighter stories following a major crash came from Gene Felton, who is one of the all-time leaders on the IMSA circuit. In the fall of 1984 Felton and his Camaro hit the sand-filled barrels at the end of the pit-lane barrier during a race at Riverside in California. He was doing 140 mph and the impact was devastating. He broke six ribs, his shoulder, and his back. The accident partly paralyzed his left side and doctors said it would take two years to recover. But Felton was back in competition by April of 1985.

What motivated him? Aside from the fact that at 49 he didn't feel he had two years to waste, he heard that his backers were ready to put Terry Labone into his car for selected races. If Felton needed extra motivation, that was it. As he said, "I love Terry like a brother, but there's two things I won't share: one's my lady, and the other's my race car."

For sheer guts, the story of NHRA's "Pink Lady," Shirley Muldowney, stands high atop the list of comebacks.

In June of 1984 "Cha Cha" Muldowney was in Montreal at an NHRA event. She was just finishing a qualifying run when the tube in her left front tire went flat, came out of the tire, and wrapped itself around the front spindle. She had been going at 240 mph when the Top Fuel dragster darted off the track and flew into a ditch and exploded, tumbling some 600 feet through the mud near the track before coming to a stop! The roll cage broke her lip. Her right hand was crushed and her thumb partly severed. Adding to the disaster were two compounded fractures of the right leg, a dislocated right ankle, and a severe dislocation of the left ankle.

After six operations and 14 months, the courageous lady was ready to return to the circuit to prove that she was still a champ. Muldowney had not only returned after what she considers "the worst drag-racing accident anyone ever survived," but she did it with a fierce determination that is her own unique style. It might be best summed up by what she told a reporter from *People* magazine: "Driving is a way of life for me, my bread and butter, and I'm not interested in anything else right now. I wasn't ready to give up the cockpit; I was forced out of it. The accident took a lot out of me, but it didn't kill my will to win. Anybody who's counting me out is dreaming."

Muldowney's bravery—as with all men and women who choose to find recognition in high-speed machines—is a quality that is tested every time she turns on the ignition. Fiery crashes, injuries and death have always been a part of racing and will continue to be a part of the sport. But that's really not what it's all about. That's when things go wrong. That's when the human spirit best shines.

Of all the words ever written about considering racing as a livelihood and risking everything in the bargain, few match what Niki Lauda, a world-class Formula One driver, said in his first book, *The Art and Science of Grand Prix Driving*: "Once in your lifetime you've got that decision: Do you want to practice this profession? Do you want it and all that it involves? If you ask yourself that question and if you answer in all honesty with yes, then that means you've beaten the problem—then you can't be afraid anymore because if you are, then you must have answered that question with a lie."

And few should know better than Lauda, who truly can be said to have come back from the dead. In 1976 he suffered such a severe crash during a Formula One race in Germany that a priest gave him his last rites. Nine years later he captured his fifth Grand Prix world driving championship!

FAST TRACK
PHOTOS

Racing champ Wendell Scott (left), was welcomed into the Black Athletes Hall of Fame in 1977 by Knicks coach Willis Reed (second from left). Also pictured are boxer Ike Williams and executive director of the Hall, Charles Mays.

The fantastic Formula One car.

Father and son racing champs Al Unser, Sr. and Al
Unser, Jr. are also known as Big Al and Little Al. Al, Sr.
won the Indy 500 in '87.

The Indy cars proudly display the names of their sponsors.

The Pit Crew is vitally important to the winning of any race.

A disabled car is towed from the track.

The Twelve Hours of Sebring is one of racing's most popular Endurance Races.

Drag racing is "like sitting on a stick of dynamite and racing the fuse," Drag Racing champ Shirley Muldowney once said.

This Drag Car owned by Steve Cotugno (in cockpit) has an engine from an old Navy Banshee jet fighter.

Drag Cars hit such high speeds that they need parachutes to slow them down at the finish line.

Funny Car driver Gary Burgin once had to dive out the window of his car because he was afraid it was about to catch fire.

Richard Petty (right) looks over his car's engine with his racing crew.

Auto racing has attracted increasing numbers of celebrities like Paul Newman.

In 1976, Janet Guthrie was the first woman to qualify for the Indy 500.

Oddly enough, racing cars are usually driven *to* their races on or in trucks.

Stock car racing is a sport that was born in the U.S.A.

Mario Andretti is one of the most famous names in racing. His son, Michael, broke into the Indy circuit in 1983.

Racing champ A.J. Foyt is known to many as "Super Tex." He's won the Indy 500 a record four times!

Ohioan Bobby Rahal was the big Indy winner in 1986.
He's one of the top racers today.

Not all cars can "endure" the rigors of Endurance Racing.

Managing the rough course is part of the challenge of Dirt Bike Racing.

The sky's the limit in Dirt Bike Racing.

Kenny Roberts (number two) has a slight edge through a turn on racer Freddie Spencer.

High speeds and sharp turns make Asphalt Motorcycle Racing a thrill-a-minute sport.

THE CRAZY SIDE OF RACING

Beyond the danger and cost of high-speed cars there are many kinds of racing for those who have speed in their blood—even if they're only eight years old! For these youngsters, and those older, it's the sport of go-karting. It's where many of today's drivers got their start. The go-kart uses a small gasoline engine, like those that power lawn mowers, and races on half-mile tracks or similar courses. It began in the United States in 1956 and has since become popular all over the world.

For the more experienced and daring, there's the Formula Vee and the larger Super Vee. They are built especially for the Volkswagen engine and can reach top speeds of about 100 mph! One of the pluses of this sport, which has been called the "poor man's Grand Prix" because it imitates the Formula One

Grand Prix car, is that the car comes in a kit and can be assembled at home.

Another rung up the ladder towards big-time auto racing is the scaled-down version of the Indy car. These cars are known as "midgets." They use a more powerful engine than Formula Vee and average speeds of from 80 to over 100 mph. The midget circuit is considered the prime training ground for drivers and even has a 500-mile race every year at the Indianapolis Speedrome, the "Midget 500."

The world of racing is not limited just to paved tracks or special cars. The sport known as "rally" can be sponsored by local sports car clubs or held on an international level. It is also open to almost any kind of car. But this kind of racing involves more than just speed. It is a contest of skill and map reading. There's not only a driver, but also his navigator. At the start of the race they get detailed instructions about the route—where to turn, how fast to travel, rest stops, and their final destination. There are checkpoints along the way, and if you're ahead or behind schedule you get penalties.

On the national level there are races such as "Dungeons and Dragons National," which is run on mountain and desert roads near Los Angeles, California. There are also world rallies sponsored by the FIA. Held on some of the worst roads, they include a bumpy, frozen course in Finland's Thousand Lake Rally, the narrow lanes on the island of Corsica, and go from snowbound Sweden to the mud of Africa's Ivory Coast. One of the most famous is the East African Safari, started in Kenya in 1953 and still held every year. It begins in Nairobi and goes on for four days through floods, dust, desert, rocks, and bush country full of wild animals. The craziest race, though, was the World Cup in 1970 when 99 drivers started out in Europe, took a boat to Brazil, and ended up in Mexico!

The only race that might top that—on a yearly basis—is the Mexican 1000. It unofficially got its start in 1962 when two men challenged each other to race motorcycles from one end of Baja California, Mexico, to the other. It is now open to five kinds of machines, even trucks, that compete in 31 classes. This race is run on some of the most hostile, rugged countryside imaginable and challenges not just a driver's ability but his sanity.

Back to more normal ground is the "slalom" or "gymkhana." It is another kind of "obstacle race," usually staged by sports car clubs and run on deserted parking lots. The driver must weave through a twisty course defined by bright plastic cones and not knock any over.

There's also "Figure Eight" racing where drivers race their stock cars around a course shaped like the figure 8, and the popular Pikes Peak Hill Climb, a race that is run up a 14,000-foot mountain in Colorado over more than 12 miles of dirt road. It attracts a lot of people, especially the Unser family, which boasts seven different Unsers winning 26 times in the last 47 years!

And if none of the above catches your interest you can always try the famous "demolition derby." It's a dash-em, smash-em race that is more like a modern version of jousting. All you have to do is destroy the opposition by driving your car straight into his. The winner is the *last* car running.

It doesn't get much crazier than that.

PART TWO:

MOTORCYCLE RACING, MOTOCROSS, DIRT, AND ASPHALT

MOTORCYCLE RACING—
WHAT'S WHAT

Motorcycle racing consists of three major categories: motocross, dirt, and asphalt racing.

Motocross

This style of racing is run on a closed course of hills with loose sand and bumps. There are four major classes in motocross based on the size the bike. The classes include 125cc, 250cc, 500cc, and Superbike.

Dirt Track Racing

This kind of racing uses knobby tires and is run on flat dirt tracks. The same classes of bike size are used as in motocross.

Asphalt Track Racing

The big difference here is the type of tires and course used. Asphalt bikes have smooth-tread tires known as "slicks." The tracks are similar to those used in Indy and stock car racing.

ATVs

These are three- and four-wheel fun buggies, the hottest fad in racing. They run on dirt trails and can go through streams as well. The wide tires are thick and knobby. ATV stands for "all-terrain vehicle."

FROM "WHOOP-DE-DOOS" TO SUPERBIKES

Motocross Racing

In the world of two-wheel excitement nothing comes close to matching the fun and thrills of the sport known as motocross. It is like a high-tech bronco-busting contest where staying in your seat becomes half the battle.

It is a place of screaming engines and flying dirt. It is where rider and machine are thrown savagely into the air and flung against embankments. It is a form of competition that pits the rider not only against the bike but also against the course itself. And to know what a challenge it is, all you really have to know is that most motocross tracks use the *worst* possible kind of land for the *best* part of the course. There are long hills of loose dirt, patches of loose sand, and bumps called "whoop-de-doos" that send rider and machine sailing through the air as if shot from a cannon.

The sport is popular not only in America but all around the world, where young and old alike rush to be part of this special brand of excitement. Even the name has its own unusual origin: The "moto" part of motocross comes from the French and Spanish for motorcycle and the "cross" from cross-country.

The first recorded motocross event took place in England in 1924, although it was the French who really got the sport going after the Second World War ended. Until the late 1960s, there were few in the United States who were really aware of motocross. It took the Continental Motosport Club (CMC) to get things moving. The organization was formed in Carlsbad, California, in 1967, but as CMC president Stu Peters said, "I literally got started with a bag of flags and some clipboards."

But when it did hit, it was like a thunderbolt. Instant motocross courses were created as tons and tons of dirt were hauled into football and baseball stadiums across the country. It attracted the top motocross drivers and the crowds as well. Only 10 years later the idea of "Supercross" was born. And in what was billed as the "Superbowl of Motocross." Seventy thousand fans filled the Los Angeles Coliseum to witness one of the first of these events.

The CMC motto "Race with the Best" couldn't be more true today, for there are 9000 members throughout the United States, Canada, and Mexico and over 500 events annually. The American Motorcyclist Association (AMA) also got into the motocross act in 1974 and now sponsors four motocross series in the 125cc, 250cc, 500cc, and Supercross class. But a lot of prestige and really big money comes from the CMC Golden State Nationals. It is where top riders compete in an eight-race series in three main classes—250cc, 500cc, and Superbike—for $600,000 in purses and the chance to become the Golden State Motocross National Champion.

Other than guts, motocross riders need a set of credentials that are even more important: they must be in top physical shape. And not just strong. They also need the endurance to take the many laps and the brutal pounding that each track dishes out. While some motocross riders win enough to have their own private plane, every one on the circuit has to be in A-one shape just to compete. That's why they're considered to be among the world's top athletes. This was proven when motocross riders were given a treadmill stress test. They stayed on for an average 17 minutes. This is impressive when you consider that someone 21 years old can only do it for 10 minutes and pro football players for only 14 minutes!

Dirt and Asphalt Racing

It all started back in 1885 when a German, Gottlieb Daimler, attached a gasoline engine to the front of his bicycle. But the first actual motorcycle was built in 1902 by George Hundes, of Springfield, Massachusetts. He called it the "Indian motorcycle" and a short time later the Davidson Brothers of Milwaukee, Wisconsin, introduced their first Harley-Davidson model.

That led to the founding of the AMA in 1924. It now sponsors some 4000 events a year in two major classes of racing—dirt track and asphalt.

Dirt Track Racing

Dirt track racing falls into four categories each of which requires a special riding style. The most popular is the one-mile oval, where racers reach speeds of up to 130 mph as they tuck in close to their gas tanks on the straights and then pitch into classic three-point slides in the turns. They stay incredibly close to the rider in the lead and photo finishes involving a pack of three to six racers are common.

The strategy is a bit different for the half-mile. Speeds are lower and a more aggressive style is required to pass another competitor, so riders hang it all out to get in front and stay there. Short-track races, run on dirt ovals only $\frac{1}{10}$ to $\frac{1}{4}$ mile in length, have their own special brand of problems. With a full field of 60 riders competing for space, the "shorts" are famous for shoulder-to-shoulder action as riders try to grab the choice spot going into a turn.

The most difficult style and truest test of rider and machine could easily be the steeplechase. There are right and left turns and one or more jumps! These machines are also fitted with a front brake, something that isn't needed on other dirt tracks. That's because a big part of the steeplechase is sliding into turns to stay in front and extra braking power is needed.

One feature common to all four styles is that the large starting fields—48 to 60 riders—are narrowed down by a series of 10-lap heats. That leaves only 15 to 17 riders to compete in the longer, main event of the day.

Asphalt Track Racing

Unlike the dirt bike circuit, AMA asphalt track racing is more often called "road racing" because it uses some of the same tracks as CART's Indy cars, such as Laguna Seca in California and Pennsylvania's Pocono Raceway. And in recent years top speeds have compared even to Grand Prix's exotic Formula One machines.

Of the several racing classes for various kinds of bikes, the premier class is Superbike, where speeds reach over 100 mph. This is the class that determines the National Road Racing Championship and uses either two-cylinder or four-cylinder engines. It's the kind of race where riders dive into corners, using special skid pads on their knees, and are only blurs of color speeding down the straightaways. And nowhere is this fast-paced world of spills and thrills better displayed than at the season's opener, a 200-mile race that attracts hundreds of thousands of fans to Daytona Beach in what has become known as the "Indianapolis of Motorcycle Racing."

Overall, the highlight of every season is the Camel Pro Series, a 30-event schedule of both dirt track and asphalt racing. It's where the top riders vie for the AMA Grand National titles and almost half a million dollars in prize money. It's also where the drivers—for dirt and asphalt—compete for the coveted "number 1 plate" that the winners can carry on their bikes all the next year.

Other riders also get a chance to show off a special colored plate. Green is worn in the Novice Division and yellow in the Juniors. Then comes the best of all, the white plate. But according to the AMA point system, only the top riders in the country are awarded numbers 1 through 99. It means that you're an "expert" and have raced with the best in the world!

CATCH THE RIDERS

Of all the stars in the motocross Milky Way, none shines brighter than veteran **Roger DeCoster**. He probably has enough trophies to decorate his den several times over. To go along with this are a very impressive five world championships in the 500cc class. It's one of the reasons that the man who was born in Belgium in 1945 is the "unchallenged king of the sport."

He is one of the most respected men in motocross and is now the coordinator for Team Honda, considered the best on the circuit and definitely the team to beat in 1987. He not only advises the bikers at the race, but has the ability to spot the little things that often make all the difference in winning or losing. That goes for the riders as well as the bikes.

It's no accident, then, that DeCoster's team dominated the world of motocross in 1986. It featured four men, three of whom can boast of individual honors in addition to being part of the number 1 motocross team.

Top gun on the team is **Rick Johnson**. He won the 1986 250 National and Supercross Championships and was second in the 500 National Championship. He also accumulated enough points throughout the season to be awarded the number 1 plate in motocross!

The number 2 man in the sport is teammate **David Bailey**. He finished second in the 1986 Supercross Championship and second in the 250 Championship. But he may soon shed runner-up status as his victory in the 1986 500 National Championship proved. The third member of the team is **Mickey Dymond**. He's the new man on the team but can still claim a championship title with his winning the 1986 125 National Championship. It was little surprise that the team which won every major category championship destroyed the competition in the Motocross des Nations, which is held in Italy.

In 1987, the fourth member of that team will be wearing the colors of Team Suzuki. **Johnny O'Mara's** move, in fact, was the biggest news of the season. He is a former champion and marathon runner who had problems in 1986 with a severe knee injury but still managed to come in third in the 250 and Supercross Grand Nationals and fourth in the 500. One of the chief reasons for the move was salary. He will be missed by his teammates. As Honda Team Coordinator DeCoster said, "I feel bad, having to let go of a guy as good as Johnny. He was the third place guy on our team this year (1986), which doesn't sound good. Still, he is one of the best riders in the world, definitely in the top four or five. I wish he could have stayed."

In dirt and asphalt (road) racing, the big names belong to **Fred Merkel** and **Bubba Shobert**. Merkel is the 1986 AMA Road Racing Series Champion. The Huntington Beach, California native also has won three consecutive AMA Superbike titles. He began his racing career in 1981 and was ranked third in the nation that year. Today he is recognized as one of the country's top talents.

Bubba Shobert is not only the 1986 AMA Dirt Track Series Champion but also the only rider to finish in the top ten in both asphalt and dirt competition. He won the dirt track title in 1985 and is the top money earner since 1980 with almost $150,000 in point bonus money alone. He also is one of only three men in AMA history to have achieved a grand slam by winning at least one of every kind of Grand National race. That includes road race, mile, half-mile, short track, and steeplechase.

Other dirt track notables include **Scott Parker** (ranked second in 1986), **Doug Chandler**, **Chris Carr**, and **Rickey Graham**. They were ranked, respectively, number 2, 3, 4, and 5 in the country. There are, of course, other top racers in the field who have made their mark in the sport. One of the best is **Jay Springsteen**, who had no 1986 national wins but holds the record as the winningest rider in AMA history with 40 career victories to his credit. There's also **Hank Scott**, who was ranked eighth in 1986 but holds the honor for posting the first official 100-mph lap on a one-mile track in AMA history. The date was July 30, 1980, at the Illinois State Fairgrounds and the official speed was 100.956 mph!

The top AMA road racing cyclists after Merkel are **Wayne Rainey**, **Randy Renfrow**, **Kork Ballington**, and **Russell Paulk**. Between them they won 12 major races in the Superbike and Grand Prix classes. Rainey had the most wins in the 1986 AMA/Camel Pro road racing series, but had to settle for finishing second to Merkel overall. Still, he was mighty impressive in winning five straight Superbike races and one Grand Prix race.

Ballington, the fourth-ranked rider, originally came from Durban, South Africa. He started racing at 16 and came out of retirement in 1986 to race in the AMA series for the first time in his career. He is the former 250cc and 350cc World Road Racing Champion.

The world of racing is not the exclusive property of the male breed. One of the most exciting dirt track riders on the circuit is 25-year-old **Tammy Kirk**. She had the best season of her career and added some color to AMA history in 1986 at the New Orleans Mile.

What she did was to become the first woman to ever win an AMA event by winning the last-chance qualifier heat. She also qualified for the main event four times in 1986 and finished sixth at DuQuoin for the best finish of her career.

Adding to her accomplishments is the fact that she and her father are the mechanics for her racing efforts. And when she's not racing motorcycles, she races late-model stock cars and works at a local motorcycle shop.

One of the "old pros" on the motocross circuit is **Sue Fish** of California. Nicknamed "Flying Fish," she first made her mark as a 17-year-old at the 1976 United States National Women's Motocross Championships. All she did there was to win! She is considered the undisputed champ of women's motocross and has won most of the U.S. titles in the 125cc and 250cc Expert class category.

Another woman who has made her mark in history is off-road racer **Mary McGee**. She not only rides motorcycles, but cars, trucks, and almost anything on off-road courses. That includes the tough Baja California 1000! She holds the distinction of being the first woman to ride in that race and has the satisfaction of actually finishing the race—something that few riders of either sex are able to do.

McGee was also the first woman to race in the International Motocross Series and the first to race in the Grand Prix motorcycle tournaments, averaging an impressive 90 mph on the asphalt. If all these accomplishments weren't enough, McGee added to her fame in 1976 when she, along with Indy 500 driver Janet Guthrie, drove a Toyota pickup truck across the wild desert of the Mexican peninsula in the Baja 1000. She and co-driver/mechanic Guthrie didn't win, but they were there again at the finish!

GETTING IN GEAR
Bikes and Equipment

SUITING UP

Before climbing into the saddle of a bike to face the competition there's one requirement that every rider must meet—dressing for the occasion. It's Safety Rule No. 1: no bare skin may show when you're on the track. And that means full coverage and padding from head to toe!

The first item is a racing suit. You can have your choice of the two-piece kind or one that looks like a pair of "long johns." Most are leather, but the latest type is made of a special nylon material. High-top boots are next. They fit tight and zip up to cover the legs of the racing suit. Then come the gloves and a crash helmet. Additional safety equipment is also encouraged, including "armor" (a chest protector) and pads for the back, shoulders, elbows, and knees. It doesn't guarantee that you'll find the winner's circle, but it means you will ride safely, win or lose.

For the machines that have been called the "wild mustangs" of the racing world—motocross—you'll also need shin guards, goggles, and a very special set of shocks. They are light, fast little beasts capable of taking a terrific beating as the riders of these steel horses bounce, slide, and jump along the series of obstacles that make up the usual course. They stand higher off the ground than either road racers or dirt trackers, with fenders raised high above the wheels, to protect the rider from flying clods of dirt, and knobby tires that dig into loose sand and gravel like tractor wheels. The kickstand is removed for safety in case it should come loose during a race. A heavy-duty shock absorber and a strong spring are mounted between the frame and the seat to help ease the jolts. The current standard runs to over 12 inches of bump-absorbing equipment. It's a good indication of how much punishment this form of sport dishes out!

MOTOCROSS BIKES

Motocross bikes have come a long way since the original bulky 400-pounders. In fact, it was the introduction of the lighter Honda 125cc types in the erly 1970s that helped get the sport on the world map. Today, even a big 500cc moto will weigh under 240 pounds. But Honda's not the only Japanese company to influence the sport. Of the 10 best motocross machines of all time, as rated by *Motocross Action* magazine, six spots were taken by Japan's Big Four: Honda, Yamaha, Suzuki, and Kawasaki.

Of all moto bikes, one of the most celebrated and best loved is the 125. An average machine in this class will have a one-cylinder engine but plenty of guts to crank out 20 horsepower at a top end of 11,500 rpms!

Although speed is not as important as handling in motocross, there's enough "juice" to hit 80 mph. The price is around $2000 for the 1986 Yamaha 125 model. But better yet is the 2-gallon gas tank that most manufacturers offer.

THE ATV

The nearest relative to motocross racing may well be the latest development in off-road racing, the ATV. These three- and four-wheel fun buggies, which began life as recreational vehicles around campsites, are quickly becoming the hottest fad in racing. They generally weigh around 350 pounds and use an air-cooled one-cylinder engine. The wide tires are thick and knobby for tackling tough trails and will pull machines through creeks just as well, or even do "wheelies." The price range is around $2000, but unlike a motorcycle, ATVs have a reverse gear in the five-speed transmission. They were not only good enough to win the fabled Baja California 1000 for the last six years (1981–1986) but also are the favorite of the Riverside, California Sheriff's Department, where they are used to patrol outdoor events held in remote areas—with siren, blinking lights, and all!

DIRT AND ASPHALT BIKES

As with the technology that brought about the ATV, today's bikes are the result of tremendous improvements over the years as aluminum and plastic replaced cast iron, and the once amazing speed of 12 mph has been multiplied by 10. This is especially true for motorcycles of the dirt or asphalt variety, which count on speed for success.

Dirt and asphalt bikes, of course, are bigger and much more expensive than moto or ATV bikes. And beyond the 125, 250, and 500cc engine sizes (the more cc, the faster it goes) that exist in moto, there is the top-of-the-line Superbike class. A typical machine is a streamlined mass of polished metal weighing about 600 pounds. Its engine is either two or four cylinders and from 750 to 1000cc. It packs a 119-horsepower wallop, goes from 0 to 60 in less than three seconds, and can do a quarter-mile at 124 mph! While most are cooled by air, some engines have liquid cooling and also feature the most advanced ideas in racing, such as fuel injection and oil coolers.

Under AMA rules, asphalt Superbike racing is limited to machines based on production-line motorcycles much like the ones fans drive to tracks. But to be truly competitive a $4000 base-price bike must undergo many hours of fine tuning and the addition of extra racing parts. With the skyrocketing cost of such racing kits ($12,000 for Honda's complete race package and $5000 for a Yamaha racing engine alone), even the best rider hopes for a spot on a "factory works" team sponsored by a major company. Without it, a rider may have to shell out as much as $25,000 to compete. The prices go even higher in the Grand Prix class, which uses bikes designed only for racing and where no expense is spared to gain power and performance.

While in Superbike and Grand Prix racing the machines must remain "stock" right down to the headlights and taillights, a dirt bike can be stripped down to the bare necessities, much like stock cars. Dirt bike racing is not a sport that is totally dominated by the Japanese manufacturers. There the standout is the American-made Harley-Davidson. Harley has stacked up an astounding 341 AMA Grand National wins since 1954, against 93 for Yamaha and 89 for Honda, with two bikes from England (Triumph and BSA) trailing far behind. But that record may be in jeopardy as Honda racked up 31 of its 89 Grand National wins in 1986 alone!

10

TWO WHEELS vs. FOUR—
Which is Most Exciting?

To begin with, comparing a car with a motorcycle is about the same as comparing an apple and an orange. But while the differences are obvious, they do share some things when it comes to the track. As auto racing great Bobby Allison has said, "As far as physical strain is concerned . . . high speeds cause tension and mental strain that can be as wearing as physical exertion." This is true at the Indy 500 or in a Motocross Grand National. As motorcyclist Ted West says, "It's a keen-edged, hyper-alert thing, somewhat similar to hot-lapping a car on a race track."

In both sports, the bike and car share the same "cornering line" on a track, meaning the rider or driver follows the same path into and out of a high-speed turn, the one that will give him that added edge over the competition in reaching the straight-away at the highest possible speed. Auto racers do it with an expert touch on the steering wheel while the motorcycle rider leans the bike over. West calls it "thrilling, throwing the bike over in each corner, holding it down . . . rolling on the power . . . like banking a plane at top speed." Driving either machine fast means knowing just how fast it can go before the tires lose their grip. And there is no margin for error.

But while fans of both sports could argue far into the night about which is more exciting to watch, there is little debate when it comes to the danger. It's worst in a car. The main reason is that even though the motorcycle rider isn't protected by a couple of tons of metal or a roll bar, he is usually thrown clear when an accident happens. In fact, riders don't wear safety harnesses for that reason. Being thrown clear of a few hundred pounds of raging machine and wearing a crash helmet and enough padding usually means avoiding serious injury. Or, as *Cycle* magazine's Paul Gordon says: "The guy's away from the bike, he's got all the right safety equipment on, everything's just fine . . . ."

On close inspection, the positives and negatives of the modern race car and the finest racing motorcycle seem to balance each other out. An Indy car may shatter lap speed records of better than 200 mph, yet the engine has to be started by a separate remote battery. A NASCAR stock car will snake in and out of a tight situation on the track, but its steering is adjusted for the two left-hand turns on an oval track and a hard turn to the right would be difficult. On the other hand, all motorcycle engines start with either a kick pedal or an electric starter button and most bikes will go across rough country that would stop any kind of car ever built. But racing a motorcycle in the rain is like tempting fate, while at 200 mph in a Grand Prix Formula One machine there isn't even a need for windshield wipers: at that speed raindrops don't stay on the windshield long enough to make a difference!

From the fans' point of view, the thrills of both styles of racing are equal. At the stock car "hot tracks" like Darlington and Atlanta, it's the almost deafening roar of the awesome engines as the green flag drops and a combined total of a few thousand horsepower leaps away from the starting line.

In motocross the pitch of sound goes up and down as riders crank the throttles over the first hill, hanging in midair, defying gravity itself. On AMA dirt tracks the pack flies past in a blast of exhaust and a cloud of dust, while at NHRA meets the pop of a dragster's parachute brings all the fans in the stands to their feet.

So, what's better might just be what you like more. Except for one fact. Motor sport, in all its many forms, from go-karts to ATVs and from Indy to Baja, is here to stay. For when the announcer's voice first boomed over the loudspeaker at Indianapolis those many years ago and said, "Gentlemen, start your engines," he spoke to generations of racers and fans everywhere for all time.

PART THREE:
EXTRA GEARS

THE CHAMPIONS

INDY CARS

CART CHAMPIONS

1986 Bobby Rahal
1985 Al Unser, Sr.
1984 Mario Andretti
1983 Al Unser, Sr.
1982 Rick Mears
1981 Rick Mears
1980 Johnny Rutherford
1979 Rick Mears
1978 Tom Sneva
1977 Tom Sneva

INDY 500 WINNERS

1986 Bobby Rahal
1985 Danny Sullivan
1984 Rick Mears
1983 Tom Sneva
1982 Gordon Johncock
1981 Bobby Unser
1980 Johnny Rutherford
1979 Rick Mears
1978 Al Unser, Sr.
1977 A.J. Foyt

STOCK CARS

NASCAR WINSTON CUP CHAMPS

1986 Dale Earnhardt
1985 Darrell Waltrip
1984 Terry Labonte
1983 Bobby Allison
1982 Darrell Waltrip
1981 Darrell Waltrip
1980 Dale Earnhardt
1979 Richard Petty
1978 Cale Yarborough
1977 Cale Yarborough

NASCAR DAYTONA 500 WINNERS

1986 Geoff Bodine
1985 Bill Elliott
1984 Cale Yarborough
1983 Cale Yarborough
1982 Bobby Allison
1981 Richard Petty
1980 Buddy Baker
1979 Richard Petty
1978 Bobby Allison
1977 Cale Yarborough

WORLD GRAND PRIX CHAMPS

1986 Alain Prost, France
1985 Alain Prost, France
1984 Niki Lauda, Austria
1983 Nelson Piquet, Brazil
1982 Keke Rosberg, Finland
1981 Nelson Piquet, Brazil
1980 Alan Jones, Australia
1979 Jody Scheckter, South Africa
1978 Mario Andretti, United States
1977 Niki Lauda, Austria

KNOW THE RACING FLAGS

Green: Start the race
Blue with Orange Stripe: Allow faster cars to pass
Black: Go immediately to the pits
Yellow: Caution on the track
Red: Stop the race
White: Last lap
Checkered: End of race

ORGANIZATIONS

There are many auto racing and motorcycle racing organizations to help the beginning racer get started on a professional career in motor sports. We've included a few you can write to for information. While you are waiting for an answer, check your local library and newsstand for books and magazines about your favorite kind of motor racing. Also, every major stock car race on NASCAR's Winston Cup circuit is televised nationwide, and network TV carries every one of the CART Indy Car World Series events. And either network television or the cable sports channel airs the highlights of NHRA drag racing and professional motocross.

Here are some of the organizations:

Championship Auto Racing Teams
390 Enterprise Court
Bloomfield Hills, MI 48013 (Indy cars)

National Hot Rod Association
Box 5555
Glendora, CA 91749 (drag racing)

National Association for Stock Car Racing
1801 Speedway Blvd.
P.O. Box Drawer K
Daytona Beach, FL 32015

Formula One Spectators Association
8033 Sunset Blvd. No. 60
Los Angeles, CA 90046 (Grand Prix)

International Motor Sports Association
860 Clinton Avenue
Bridgeport, CT 06605

American Motorcyclist Association
P.O. Box 6114
Westerville, OH 43081

American Road Racing Association
220 W. Carrillo St. No. 15
Santa Barbara, CA 93101 (motorcycles)

Continental Motosport Club
18019 Skypark Circle
Irvine, CA 92714 (motocross)

RACING SCHOOLS

There are many racing schools to choose from. The one we've included here is that of former driver Bob Bondurant. The address is:

Bob Bondurant
School of High Performance Driving
Sears Point International Raceway
Sonoma, CA 95476